MY ART BOOK

BOOK

Animals

DK

DK

LONDON, NEW YORK, MUNICH,
MELBOURNE, and DELHI

Project editor Alexander Cox
Senior designer Sonia Moore
Editor Lorrie Mack
US editor Margaret Parrish
Designers Gemma Fletcher, Rosie Levine,
Lauren Rosier

Photographer Will Heap
Art consultant Ian Chilvers
Picture researcher Jo Walton
Production editor Siu Chan
Production controller Kara Wallace
Jacket designer Rosie Levine
Publishing manager Bridget Giles
Creative director Jane Bull
Category publisher Mary Ling

First American Edition, 2012
Published in the United States by
DK Publishing
375 Hudson Street, New York, New York 10014

12 13 14 15 16   10 9 8 7 6 5 4 3 2 1
001–182768–05/12

A catalog record for this book
is available from the Library of Congress.
ISBN: 978-0-7566-9275-9

DK books are available at special discounts when
purchased in bulk for sales promotions, premiums,
fund-raising, or educational use. For details, contact:
DK Publishing Special Markets, 375 Hudson Street, New
York, New York 10014 or SpecialSales@dk.com.

Printed and bound in China
by Hung Hing

Discover more at
www.dk.com

CONTENTS

Take a walk on the wild side of art
and discover these amazing animal
masterpieces inside!

Discover how to paint, sculpt,

engrave, draw, model, and create amazing animal art!

Scale

To show how large or small a piece of art is we have compared it to this hand or child.

The child is 43 in (110 cm) tall.

The hand is 5 in (12 cm) high.

FOREWORD

Children are naturally curious about the world around them. *My Art Book: Animals* creates the opportunity to indulge a child's curiosity, and encourages the importance of making time for creativity. It does so with the simple premise that animals are an inspiration to artists and all people throughout history.

The gallery pages, arranged around famous artists and their animal inspirations, serve as a virtual museum for children that they can visit anytime, while the artist and art project pages provide prompts for discussion, discovery, and interpretation. The step–by–step instructions create a hands–on classroom—the perfect formula for visual learning. Children can work at their own pace, review, and relate their projects to the illustrated examples.

Children are fearless and fun. With a little guidance and materials at the ready, you'll be amazed at the art they will create, whether you have a formal area in your home for making art, or if you just push back the tablecloth and lay down some newspaper.

With an array of animals as diverse and unique as each of the young readers who will open its pages, *My Art Book: Animals* is sure to inspire young artists to appreciate art, interact with it, and create their own amazing works of animal art.

Renée Collins
Artist/Art Educator

Walls of art

THE ANCIENT EGYPTIANS painted pictures on the interior walls of tombs. They surrounded the dead with familiar scenes to guide and help them in the afterlife. This fresco shows the cattle of Egyptian nobleman Nebamun being presented for inspection.

The hieroglyphs behind the farmers tell the story of how the farmers argued as they moved through the line.

The cattle are shown in five layers and the Egyptian artists use different colors to separate the images.

Cattle Brought For Inspection
Unknown artist, **c. 1350 BCE**,
wall painting (fresco)

The fresco is this **big!**

Cats were originally wild animals, but were domesticated by the ancient Egyptians.

Egypt and animals

The cat was a sacred animal to the ancient Egyptians. They worshiped it because of its skill at killing vermin, such as rats and snakes. The Egyptians respected their cats so much that families would mummify their favorite animals after they died.

Draw like an Egyptian

The ancient Egyptian artists were more interested in clarity than accuracy. They drew the human body facing forward, but the head in side view. Animals were drawn side on and some features, such as eyes, were made larger to give the drawings more impact.

This artwork is one of a few fragments that remain from the tomb of Nebamun. The paint has survived for thousands of years in Egypt's dry climate.

The Egyptians also worshiped animal-headed gods. These included, lions, hawks, crocodiles, and even a frog.

PAINTS & PLASTER

! Avoid skin contact when handling plaster.

You will need:

Light plaster
Mixing bowls
A jar of water
Foil container
Wooden spoon
Color pastels
Sandwich bags
Paint brushes

A foil container is essential (plastic containers may melt).

Making plaster

This project uses light plaster, which is tricky to mix and must be handled with care, so ask an adult to help and avoid skin contact with the plaster. Light plaster dries very quickly, so it's a good idea to get everything ready before you begin.

1 Choose the colors you want to use on your fresco. Place each pastel in a separate bag and carefully crush the pastels with a wooden spoon.

2 Read the mixing and safety instructions on the back of the light plaster and ask an adult to carefully mix the required amount with water.

3 As you mix the plaster, pour in the crushed pastel of your chosen background color and stir it into the plaster mix.

4 After you have mixed the plaster, carefully pour it into the foil tray and smooth the top with the back of a spoon. You can sink a knotted piece of string into the wet plaster so you can hang up your fresco once it's finished.

5 While the plaster dries make sure you have all your pastels crushed, and pour a couple of spoonfuls of plaster into the jar of water.

6 Pour your crushed pastels into separate bowls and mix the powdered pastel with some of the plaster water to make a wet paste.

7 Using your chosen color, paint the outline of your animal. You can add more water to the pastel paste if it gets too dry.

8 Build up the colors on your fresco one by one. The pastel paint will dry slowly, so be careful not to smudge or mix the colors.

Finishing touches

To make your fresco look like it's been discovered inside an Egyptian tomb, add details like hieroglyphs and Egyptian patterns.

BURIAL SCENES

In ancient Egypt, fine tomb frescoes honored important people after their deaths.

Tomb of Tutankhamun

This baboon detail comes from one of the many animal scenes in the tomb of the famous boy pharoah.

Tomb of Menna

Menna was a scribe (clerk) to Tuthmoses IV, so he was important enough to have a grand tomb adorned with images like this fishing scene.

Tomb of Nefermaat

This is part of a long thin image showing six geese in all. They are so finely painted that experts think Nefermaat must have been royal.

Tomb of Sennedjem

The man this tomb was made for was not royal, but his tomb was extremely fine. Here, the god Isis (below), disguised as a falcon, stands guard.

Tomb of Sennedjem

Here, Sennedjem is using two dappled (spotted) oxen to sow grain in the blessed fields of the afterlife.

Tomb of Nekhtamun

Ra, the Sun god, is shown in the form of a cat, killing the serpent god Apophis.

Wooden rhino

Rhinoceros
by Albrecht Dürer, **1515**
Print from woodcut

ALBRECHT DÜRER (1471-1528) was a German painter and printmaker. His prints were produced in large numbers, spreading his fame across Europe.

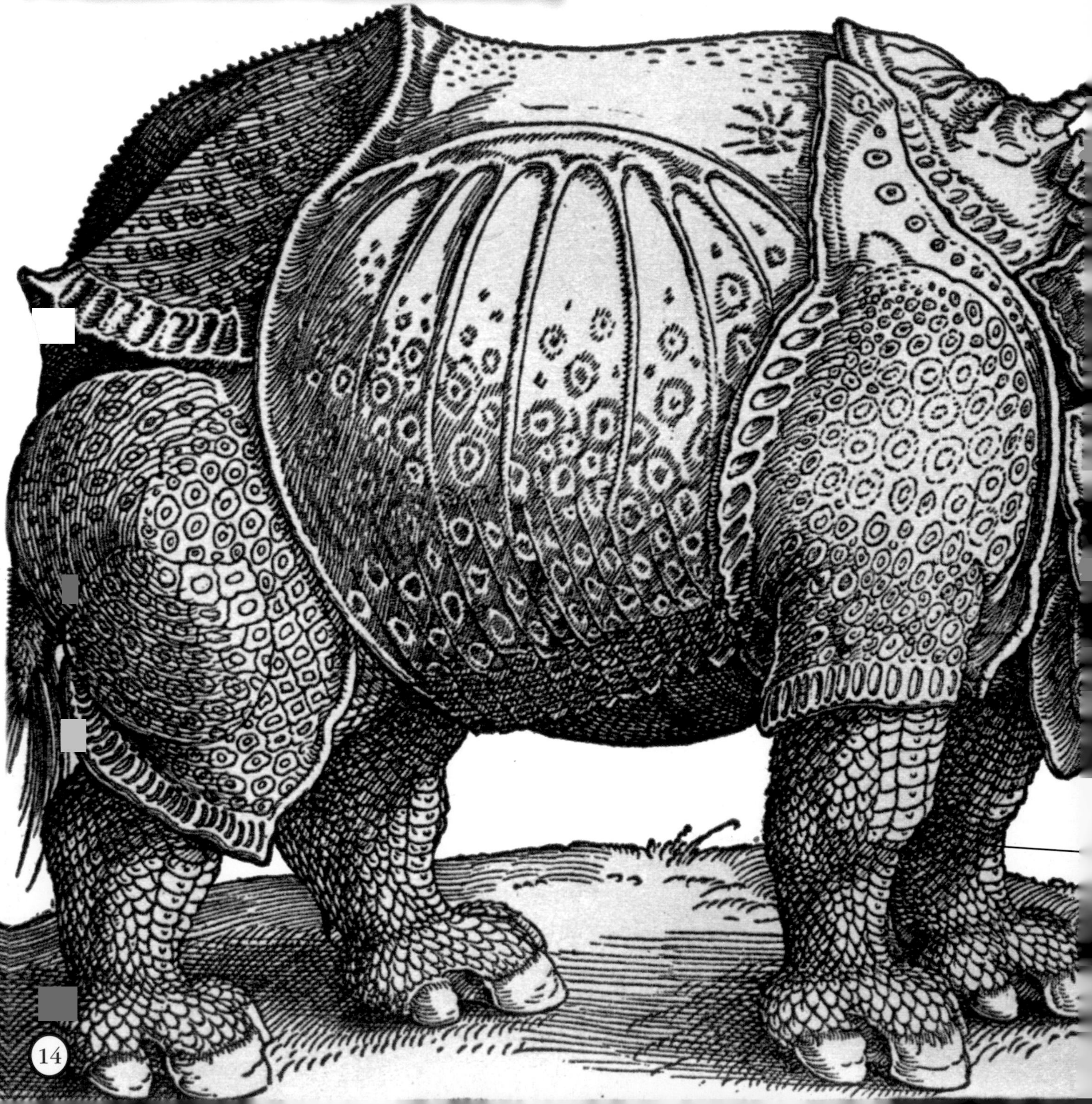

The print is this **big!**

Can you spot the differences between Dürer's *Rhinoceros* and a real rhinoceros?

Self Portrait
Albrecht Dürer, 1500

Wood Cutter

Artist

Dürer was one of the main artists of the Northern Renaissance era. Many of his famous artworks are woodcuts. These were made by carving the image onto the surface of a smooth wooden block. The block was then coated in ink so a print on paper could be made.

Rhinoceros sighting

Dürer never actually saw a real rhinoceros. He created his *Rhinoceros* woodcut from a written description and an illustration of the first rhinoceros seen in Europe for about one thousand years.

An Indian rhinoceros

Creative anatomy

Dürer's woodcut of the rhinoceros remained the main reference illustration for hundreds of years, even though the image was more fanciful creation than accurate animal art. Dürer's *Rhinoceros* has tortoiseshell armor that seems to be riveted in place, scaly legs, and an extra horn on its back.

Dürer gave his rhinoceros scales like a lizard.

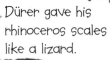

Dürer took inspiration from the world around him, and he added a kind of "gorget" to his rhinoceros. This was a piece of neck armor worn by knights of the period.

You will need:

Foil tray
Masking tape
Scissors
Tracing paper
Pens
Wooden skewer
Black paint and brush

1 Find an image of a tortoise and, using tracing paper, trace the outline of the animal.

2 Cut the foil tray so it's the same size as your traced tortoise. Tape the tracing paper securely to the foil.

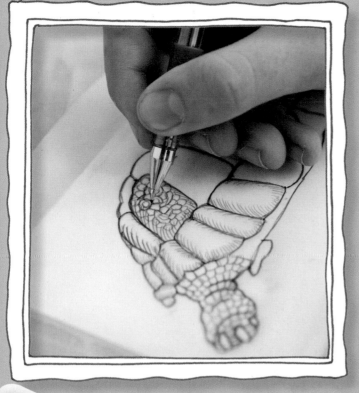

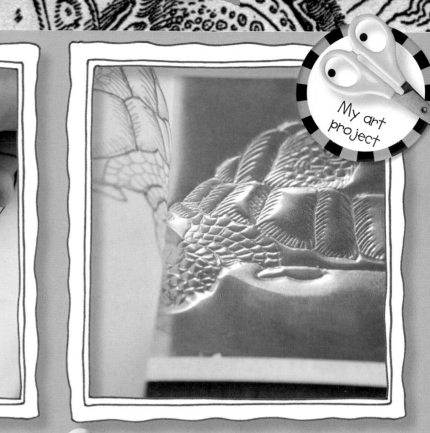

3 Using a black pen, press firmly and draw over the outline of the tortoise. With a different color pen, draw detail onto the tortoise shell, feet, and head.

4 Every now and again check the foil to see how your tin tortoise is looking. Be careful not to move the tracing paper or the foil out of place.

5 Once you have filled in all the detail, remove the tracing paper and you have a cool engraving of a tin tortoise!

Why not trace Dürer's Rhinceros and turn it into a tin engraving!

Frame your finished piece or stick it onto a notebook to make a shiny cover.

As a finishing touch, you can paint around your tin engraving and scratch patterns into the paint with a wooden skewer.

My art project

LIFE DRAWING

Dürer was the first great artist to be fascinated by the whole animal kingdom.

A Young Hare 1502

This little animal looks alert, as if it could jump up at any second, but experts think Dürer painted it from a stuffed model.

The Little Owl 1508

Look at the bottom of this picture, on the left—can you find Dürer's special monogram, or signature? It's a little "D" inside a big "A."

Wing of a Roller 1512

When Dürer was alive, lots of new animals and plants were being found all over the world. The bright roller bird whose wing he depicted here was exotic and exciting in 1512.

Squirrels 1512

Dürer painted these hungry nibblers in a type of watercolor called gouache. This is especially thick, so the paper doesn't show through.

Head of a Roe Deer 1514

This small, reddish-brown deer, which is well suited to Germany's cold winters, is still common in Europe and Asia.

Monkey *date unknown*

Experts think Dürer painted this monkey, but they're not absolutely sure, so they say it's "attributed" to him.

Mane man

PETER PAUL RUBENS (1577-1640) was known as the "prince of painters and painter of princes." He was the most famous, versatile, and successful artist of his time.

Daniel in the Lions' Den by Peter Paul Rubens, **1615**, oil on canvas

The big picture

Daniel was counselor to King Darius. The king's other ministers were jealous and had Daniel locked in a lions' den. The next morning, when Darius moved the entrance stone, he found Daniel safe and giving thanks to God.

The painting is this **big!**

Artist

Most of the things in this picture are brown—such as the fur on the animals, and the large areas of rock. Against all this brown, Daniel's pale skin and red robe stand out, so you look at him first.

Perfect practice

Before they produce oil paintings, many artists make drawings of what they want to show. Rubens did this drawing of a lioness in colored chalks—can you see the finished animal in his painting?

Royal Rubens

Named after two saints, Peter Paul Rubens was born in Siegen (Germany), but lived most of his life in Flanders (Belgium). A scholar who spoke several languages, he painted pictures for royal and noble families across Europe. Rubens loved ancient sculpture, and he exchanged a number of his works for a collection of Roman statues.

Self Portrait
Peter Paul Rubens, 1623

KING OF MASKS

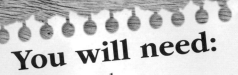

You will need:
Cardboard
Chalk
Masking tape
Scissors
Paper bags and envelopes
Craft glue
Paint brush and paints

1 Make sure your piece of cardboard is big enough to cover your face and sketch a lion's face on it in chalk.

2 Use a paper bag or envelope to make a nose. You can pad the nose out with scrap paper.

3 Carefully cut out your lion's face and secure the lion's nose using strips of masking tape.

4 Fold some paper bags into thirds lengthwise, then fold into an accordion shape. Cut along the folds to create strips, leaving a few inches uncut at the top.

5 To make the mane curly, wrap the strips around a paint brush, then unwind. For effect, curl the top layer more than the bottom layer.

6 To make the lion's ears, cut large circles out of a paper bag. Hold the bottom of the circle and pinch it together, as shown.

7 Position the ears on your mask and glue in place. You can also use masking tape to make sure they are attached securely.

8 To make your headband, cut some cardboard into long strips. Wrap the headband around your head to make sure it fits, then tape it to the mask. The support strip sits on top of your head.

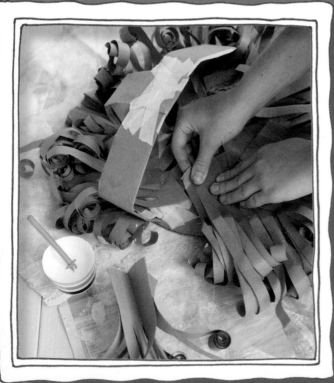

9 You can now add your mane to your mask. Repeat steps 4 and 5 so you have lots of curly mane sections and glue them to the inside of the mask.

10 Use yellow, orange, and red to paint the lion's face. Then use black paint to emphasize the eyes, nose, and mouth.

Cover the inside of the mask with an oval piece of cardboard, so you don't scratch your face on the mane.

Make two eye holes in the mask using a sharp pencil and a lump of sticky tack.

Why not paint some yellow detail on the ends of the curly mane? You are now ready to show off your new mask... ROAR!

TOUCH OF GENIUS

Rubens treated every subject brilliantly—his animals look as if they might come alive.

These cherub-bearing lions suggest power and strength. They also make a visual joke on "Lyon" in France, which is where the king and queen first met.

Can you find the mouse?

This story (below right) just might be true—when restorers cleaned the picture recently, they found overpainting on the mouse. They removed it!

The Lion and the Mouse c. 1620

Rubens created this scene with his friend Frans Snyders. It once hung in the country house of Winston Churchill, an avid amateur artist—according to one story, he couldn't see the mouse clearly, so he touched it up!

Tiger Hunt *c.* 1617

Rubens' studio produced lots of enormous, crowded hunting scenes—this one is more than 10ft (3m) wide! Rubens could never have seen some of the exotic animals he painted, so he probably worked from stuffed models.

Parrot *c.* 1630

Rubens had lots of other artists working for him. Experts think one of them painted this with Rubens' guidance.

Portrait of Giovanni Carlo Doria on Horseback *c.* 1606

Doria was an important Italian nobleman. To reflect his great power and influence, Rubens painted him on a charging steed.

Horse power

ALTHOUGH HE BEGAN his career producing portraits of people, George Stubbs (1724-1806) is now famous as the greatest horse painter of all time. This portrait is by Ozias Humphry.

Life studies

After studying human anatomy (what's inside bodies), Stubbs turned his attention to horses. In 1766, he published his famous book, *The Anatomy of the Horse*, creating all the illustrations himself. He knew horses better than any other artist and painted them with great energy, like the white one shown here. The lion looks a bit lifeless, though—Stubbs probably used the stuffed trophy from an exotic hunt as his model.

Time to learn

In order to learn all about horses' bodies, Stubbs spent 18 months in the English countryside, drawing as many animals as he could, and cutting up dead ones.

The inspiration for this scene may have been a trip to Morocco, where Stubbs saw a lion attacking a horse. There is also an ancient statue with this theme, which he could have known.

A Horse Frightened by a Lion
by George Stubbs, **1770,**
oil on canvas

The painting is this big!

Wherever the idea came from, Stubbs fell in love with it—in total, he produced nearly 20 similar pictures.

DRAWING HORSES

You will need:

Black cardboard
Masking tape
Tracing paper
Color pastels
Pencil
Eraser

You can use black paper.

A Horse's body

Before you start, you need to plan your picture. Take a look at Stubbs' horse and break it down into simple shapes.

The horse's head and neck become rectangles and triangles. The body is a large rectangle with circles at the joints. Use simple lines for the legs.

1 Draw the horse shapes straight onto the black cardboard, or tape tracing paper over Stubbs' horse, copy the shapes, and transfer them onto the cardboard.

2 Using a white pastel and a stronger line, draw the outline of your horse by fleshing out the basic horse shapes.

3 Now fill in the horse using your white pastel. You can always refer back to Stubbs' horse if you need help with the detail.

Use your finger to blend the colors.

4 Use a dark grey or black pastel to add shadows to parts of the horse. Use curving strokes to show the "roundness" of the horse's belly.

As a finishing touch, blend some yellow and brown chalk to create an earth-colored ground.

BEASTS OF BEAUTY

As a painter-scientist, George Stubbs was fascinated by all wild and domestic creatures.

Fanny, a Brown and White Spaniel 1778

John Musters was one of Stubbs' most important patrons (people who commission work). Fanny was the much-loved pet of Musters' wife Sophia.

Cheetah and Stag with Two Indians c. 1765

This painting illustrates the true story of an aristocrat who ordered his servants to release a wild cat and a stag so he could watch the kill—but the stag escaped!

Warren Hastings on his American Horse 1796

The first governor-general of India, Hastings was later accused of corruption. He was cleared the year before this portrait was painted.

Whistlejacket c. 1762

This huge portrait of a famous racehorse—nearly 10ft (3m) tall—was done for its owner, the Marquess of Rockingham. Many stories are told about it—in one, the stallion was so disturbed when he saw his own image that he tried to attack it.

Portrait of a Monkey
1799

Stubbs painted this image twice, 25 years apart—this is the last version. Toward the end of his life, he planned a book of pictures comparing the bodies of humans and animals.

Zebra 1763

Today, we know there are several types of zebra. This is a mountain zebra, but it's called just *Zebra* because it was the only one known in Stubbs' time.

Holy symbol

TIPU SULTAN ruled Mysore in India from 1782 to 1799. For him, the tiger was a holy symbol of power over his enemies—he had tiger decorations on his walls, his throne, his weapons, and his soldiers' uniforms. This life-sized figure was made for Tipu Sultan.

Scary toy

Tipu's Tiger is a type of wind-up toy called an *automaton*—there's a handle coming out of the beast's shoulder (see above). When it's turned, the tiger growls and its victim cries out, lifting his hand to his mouth in terror.

The figures themselves were carved from wood, painted, then covered with shiny lacquer for protection.

Tipu's Tiger
maker unknown, *c.* 1790, *painted wooden toy*

The figure is this **big!**

Artist

Movement and music

Also concealed inside the figure is a small pipe organ. During the 1800s, when the automaton lived in the Reading Room of the East India Company Museum, students constantly grumbled when visitors wound it up and played tunes.

Weighted bellows supply wind to the mechanical organ's 18 pipes. These are operated from an ivory keyboard hidden behind a flap in the animal's side (see above).

The figure being savaged by the tiger is clearly European, but experts aren't sure if he's a soldier or an ordinary man. What do you think?

To make the tiger

This will be the tiger's body.

You will need:
1 plastic milk carton
3 paper towel rolls
4 plastic forks
Scrap cardboard
1 dome-shaped lid
Newspaper
Scissors
Masking tape

One for the front legs

Two for the back legs

Cut the paper towel rolls.

claws

for the tiger's head

cardboard to make the ears

To make the legs, you need to turn the paper towel rolls into small tubes. Cut each roll in half across its width (1), then cut the halves lengthwise (2). Now roll the halves into small thin tubes and secure with tape.

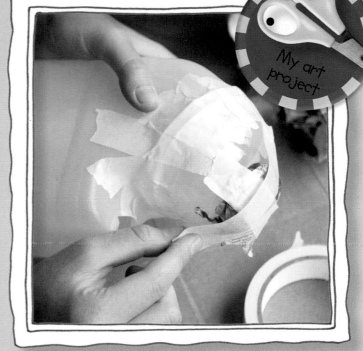

1 Cut off the milk carton's handle and top. Tape the dome-shaped lid to the carton. If you don't have a dome-shaped lid, ball up some newspaper.

2 Secure the lid to the carton with masking tape—this will be the tiger's head. For the nose, tape on a small ball of newspaper, as shown.

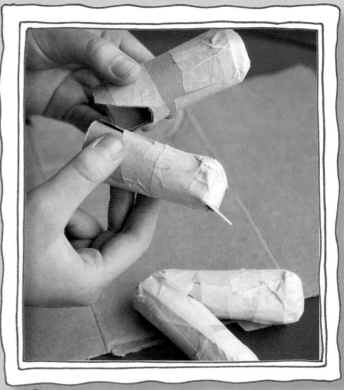

3 Draw some ear shapes on your cardboard and cut them out. Pinch the ears and tape them to your tiger's head using some masking tape.

Add claws to the legs by cutting a plastic fork in half and then sliding it into the end of the tube.

4 For the back legs, cut a U-shape into one cardboard tube, as shown, and tape the joint together. Fill the legs with newspaper to make them solid.

37

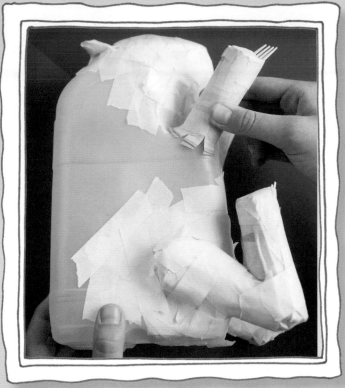

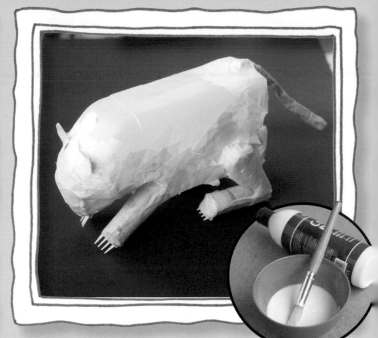

5 Attach the rear legs using masking tape. To attach the front legs, cut ½in (1cm) slits into the attaching end and tape onto the carton, as shown.

6 Roll up a long strip of newspaper for the tail and attach it to the carton. To finish, brush on a layer of watered-down craft glue.

7 Once the craft glue is dry, you can start painting the tiger. Start with an orange base coat, then add the black tiger stripes.

8 Finally, paint the face detail onto the tiger and give it a big growling mouth and wide scary eyes!

Your finished tiger should look like this.

My art project

You will need:
1 candy box
1 aluminum foil roll
2 plastic teaspoons
flexible drinking straws
1 lemon squeeze-bottle
Scrap cardboard
Scissors
Masking tape

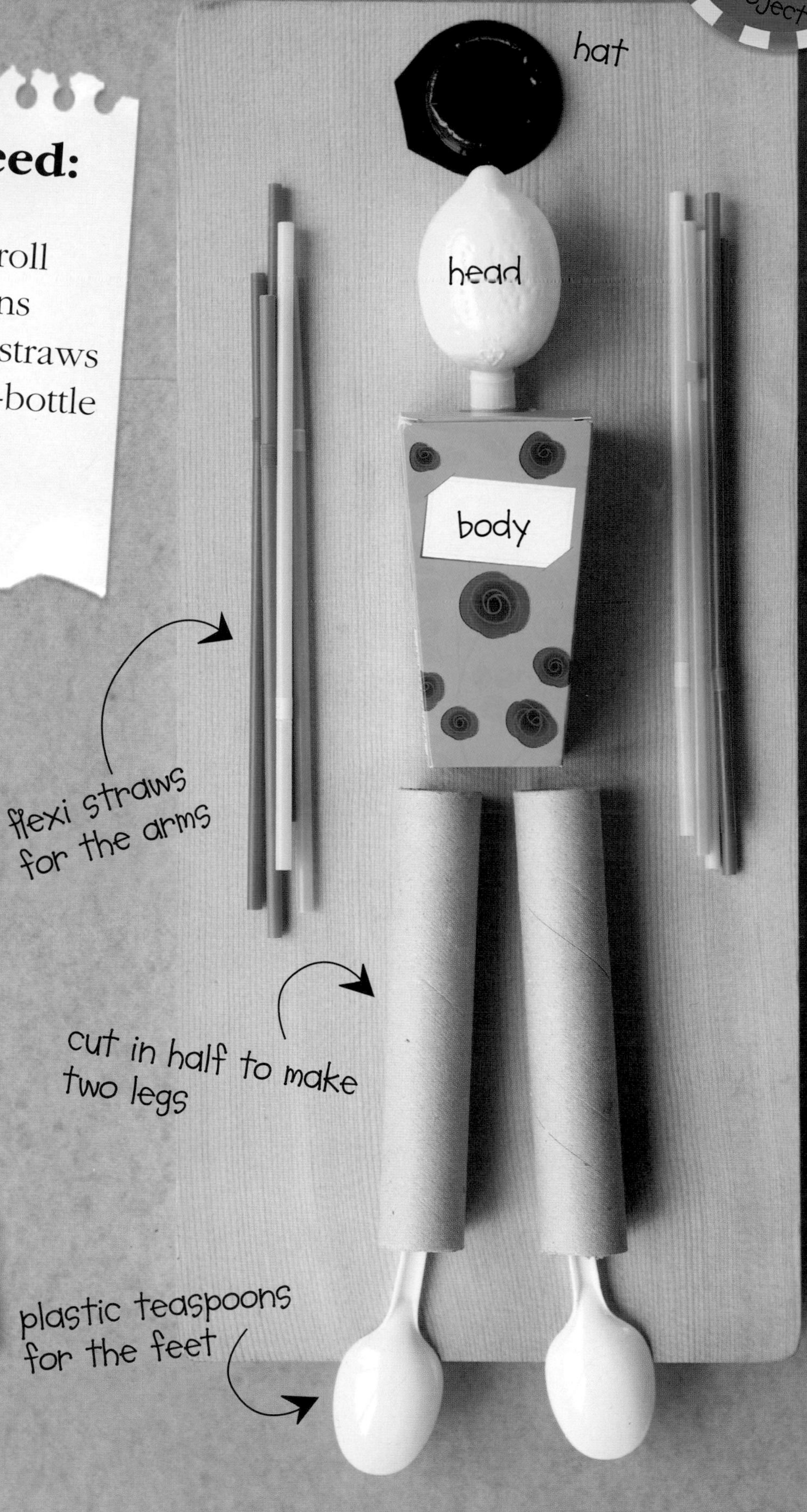

hat

head

body

flexi straws for the arms

cut in half to make two legs

plastic teaspoons for the feet

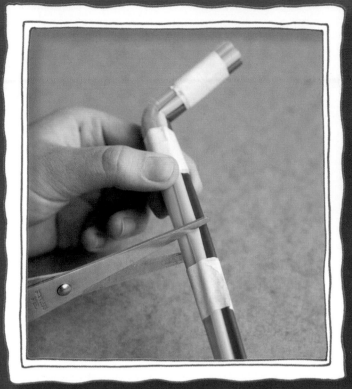

9 Cut the handle off the spoon and tape the spoon to the paper towel roll, as shown. Repeat with the other spoon and roll to make two legs with feet.

 10 For the arms, tape together about five straws and cut to size. The bendable ends will form the man's elbow joint.

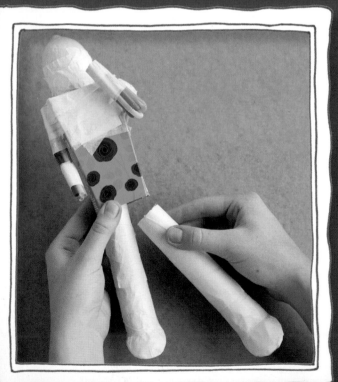

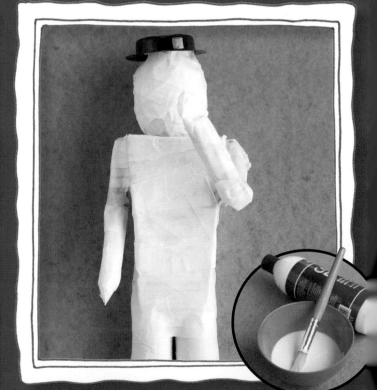

11 Carefully attach the legs and arms to the candy-box body. Tape the lemon squeeze-bottle to the top of the candy box to make the man's head.

12 Cover the whole man with masking tape and paint him with a coat of watered-down craft glue. Add the hat to the top of the man's head.

 13 When the craft glue is dry, your man is ready to paint. Use red for the jacket, and paint the pants black. Remember to paint his shoes and socks.

 14 Finally, paint the detail on to the man's scared face. Once the paint is dry, you can stick the tiger on top of the man with some glue.

STARRY STRIPES

Tigers, the biggest of all jungle cats, have always attracted the artist's eye.

Tasmanian Tiger #3 1989

American artist William L. Hawkins used shiny enamel paints for his bold figures. He worked from pictures in books and magazines.

Tiger 1966

Rosina Becker do Valle didn't start painting until she was in her 40s. Most of her work concentrates on the forests and folk stories of her native Brazil.

Henri Rousseau's Dream Garden 1997

Rousseau was a French painter who featured tigers and jungles in his work. In this picture, artist Frances Anne Bloomfield imagines him in his own fantasy landscape.

Tiger Shaking Head 1996

Odile Kidd was born in southern Africa, and her work concentrates on the area's wildlife. This life-sized image brings out the beast's expression and personality.

Digital Origami Tiger 2010

To mark the Chinese year of the tiger, two of these digitally designed figures toured the world. Inspired by origami (Asian paper folding), they were made from lots of different— recyclable—materials.

Tiger (from life) 1886

This print is based on an earlier (1803) silk painting by Japanese artist Kiuho Toyei. At this time, Japanese culture stressed how unimportant humans are, which is why nature subjects were so popular.

Living colors

FRANZ MARC (1880-1916) was a German Expressionist artist. For him, animals represented innocence, and he used bold shapes and bright colors to try to show how they might feel rather than how they look.

The Red Bull
by Franz Marc, **1912,**
watercolor on paper

The painting is this big!

Man of the spirit

Franz Marc was a very religious man, and at one time he wanted to become a priest. He thought people were too worried about money and power, which is why he cared so much for animals. When World War I broke out, he joined the army, and he later died in the fighting.

"The feel for life in animals made all that was good in me come out." **FRANZ MARC**

Why do you think Franz Marc painted his bull in such a strong red? It looks very peaceful, but do you think it's in danger?

Can you see the rough texture of the paper through Marc's paint?

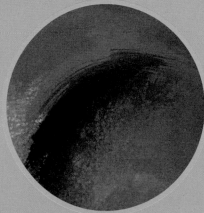

Color signals

Franz Marc usually showed animals in harmony with nature—he thought they were more beautiful and purer than humans. His bright colors had special meaning for him: blue was male and spiritual; yellow was female and gentle; and red was violent and brutal.

Animals, Franz Marc, 1913

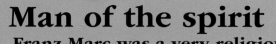

45

WAX ELEPHANTS

You will need:

Paper
Pencil
Wax crayons
Watercolor paints
Paint brushes
A cup of water

1 Using Franz Marc's graphic style as a guide, draw a simple elephant in a jungle setting.

2 With a wax crayon color of your choice, draw a thick outline around the elephant.

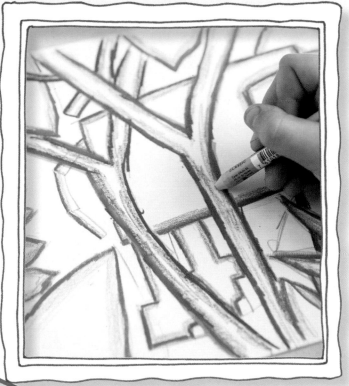

3 Draw thick outlines using different colors around your jungle setting. Add some fine detail to the bark of the trees and leaves of the plants.

4 Once you've drawn all the outlines, use the watercolors to paint inside the shapes. The crayon will stop the paint from bleeding outside the shapes.

My art project

CURVES & LINES

Some of Marc's animals have natural shapes, and some are made into split-up images.

Foxes 1913

You can clearly see the head of one fox, but the rest of the animals are broken into angular shapes.

Blue Horse 1911

Franz Marc loved blue—he helped to found a group of Expressionist painters called _Der Blaue Reiter_ (The Blue Rider).

Black and Blue Fox 1911

Marc believed that each person has the same response to individual colors, so painters can use them to express emotion. Why do you think this fox is blue?

Three Animals (Dog, Fox, Cat) 1912

In this painting, and the one of the tiger (below), you can see Marc's animals just starting to take on geometric shapes.

Tiger 1912

Here, Marc has kept the tiger's basic shape and color, but made it simpler and brighter, with angled edges—it almost looks like a big jewel sitting in a landscape of other precious stones.

Elephant, Horse, and Cow 1914

Toward the end of his life, Marc's animals were almost getting lost among his brilliant colors and broken shapes. He took this style further and further, until almost nothing in his work looked realistic.

Klee color

German artist **PAUL KLEE** (pronounced "clay") (1879-1940) was one of the leading painters of the 20th century. His paintings are lively, colorful, and witty.

Can you find me in the painting?

The colorful Klee

Klee loved, studied, and wrote about color. He began his career working in black and white. However, in 1914 he visited north Africa, and the bright sunlight awoke him to the beauty of color.

"The beholder's eye, which moves like an animal grazing, follows paths prepared for it in the picture." PAUL KLEE

Painting with scissors

Landscape With Yellow Birds started off as a different piece of art. The orange-brown trees on the left and right edges of the picture used to be one tree. Klee wasn't happy with how the painting looked, so he cut it in half and reassembled it. Klee then left a strip between the two halves and painted two yellow birds poking out of the gap.

Klee kept things looking simple, as if a child had painted the art. However, this simple look was thoroughly planned and delicately carried out.

Landscape With Yellow Birds
By Paul Klee, **1923**
watercolor

The painting is this
big!

Artist

1923 // 32 Landschaft mit gelben Vögeln.

STENCIL BIRDS

old plastic folders

You will need:
Old plastic folders
Felt-tip pen
Scissors
Black cardboard
Acrylic paints
Pieces of sponge
Paint brushes
Old erasers
Cup of water

Make sure you use thick paper or cardboard.

1 On the old plastic folders, use a felt-tip pen to draw some scenery shapes such as trees and plants. You can use Klee's *Landscape With Yellow Birds* for inspiration.

2 Make your stencils by carefully cutting out the inside of the shapes, making sure you don't cut outside the line. Lightly sponge shades of blue across the top of the cardboard for the sky.

3 Position your stencil on the black cardboard and tape it in place along the top. Using a clean sponge, dab the paint over your stencil.

4 Now add some different colors. Lift the stencil and check your progress from time to time. Once finished, carefully remove the stencil.

5 Use the other stencils to create your landscape. Hold the stencil in place with masking tape. Use a range of colors for the different shapes.

6 You can use your stencils as many times as you want. Try rotating them, or you can use different colors.

7 You are now ready to make your birds. Draw a bird body on one pencil eraser and a bird head on another, then carefully cut them out.

8 Use the eraser body and head as stamps. Dip them into yellow paint and then pick a place on your landscape and press down hard.

9 Once you have added all the yelllow birds you want, you can use a paint brush to add extra detail, such as feet, eyes, and wings.

10 As a finishing touch, use a fine paint brush to add detail to the plants and background. Use stripes and spots to break up flat colors.

FANCY FLYERS

From fat owls to graceful doves, birds appeal to artists of every kind.

Water-bird mosaic 4th century

Mosaics are pictures made by setting glass or marble chips into wet plaster. This mosaic is from an ancient empire and was found in Germany.

The Owl 1947

Pablo Picasso was inspired by the things around him, and he made several paintings of this injured owl perched on a wooden chair.

Birds *c.* 1959

Andy Warhol created this early ink drawing in the bright, clear colors he used for advertising artwork. Do you think it's about Christmas—partridges in a pear tree?

This duck family was carved by Inuits in the Arctic.

Man in a Bowler Hat 1935

For René Magritte, this bowler-hatted figure represented the common man—he painted lots of them, but he always covered the face to hide individual features. Experts think the dove symbolizes the human spirit.

Blue-Necked Bird 2002

Nancy Nicholson made this bird out of pieces of stuck-on paper. A picture like this is called a "collage."

Eagle 2001

Ex-welder Joe Pogan makes sculptures out of reclaimed materials, which artists call "found" objects.

Three Studies of a Bullfinch c. 1505

The photographic detail and formal layout of this stunning watercolor by Albrecht Dürer make it look strangely modern.

Pogan constructed his big eagle (it's 26in/66cm high) out of nuts and bolts, tools, cutlery, tokens, and brass buttons.

Fish and Shapes

Spanish artist **PABLO PICASSO** (1881–1973) started creating artwork when he was just a child. Picasso was the most famous artist of the 20th century. He made sculptures, prints, and ceramics, in addition to paintings

The painting is this big!

Artist

Legendary artist

Picasso achieved fame in his own lifetime, unlike some other great artists. He cofounded Cubism with fellow artist Georges Braque. They broke up the shapes of objects and then rearranged them decoratively on the canvas.

"Everyone wants to understand painting. Why is there no attempt to understand the song of birds?"

PABLO PICASSO

Colorful crab

The Soles was painted by Picasso while he lived in Paris, France. He took his inspiration from the small, French coastal town of Royan. Although the artwork is called *The Soles*, the fish in the painting aren't soles, and the crab is the feature that stands out the most.

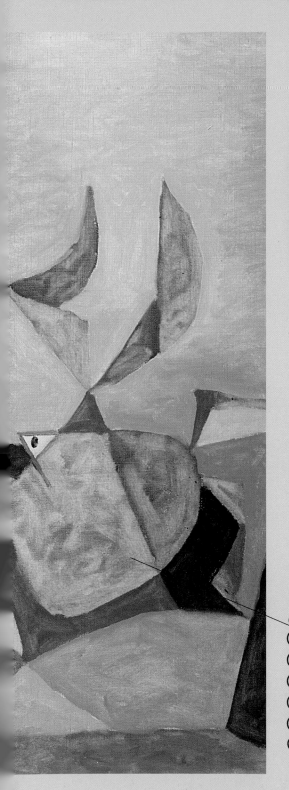

The crab shows how Picasso would simplify shapes and colors to give them more impact. It stands out clearly against the flat background.

The orange crab and its large claws reflect and balance the shape and color of the measuring scales on the left.

CRAB COLLAGE

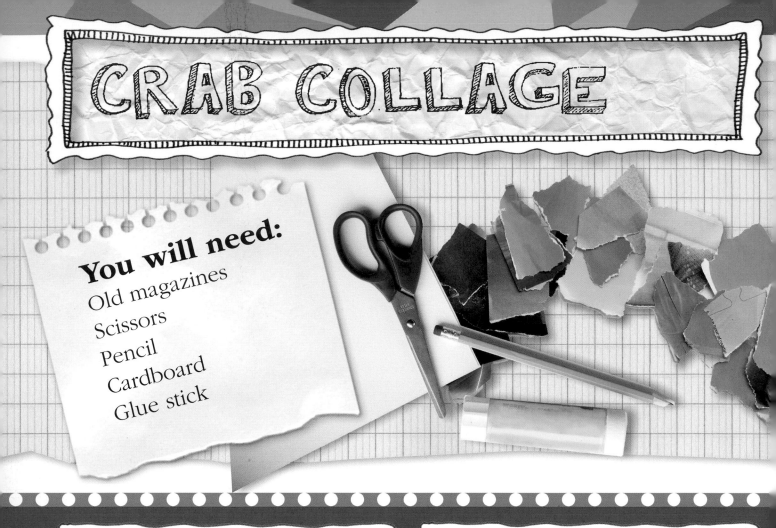

You will need:

Old magazines
Scissors
Pencil
Cardboard
Glue stick

1 Cut and rip your magazine pages into small shapes. Start the collage background by using the blue scraps. Glue them onto your cardboard.

2 Gradually build you background with different tones of blue and try to create curves and bands of shape and color.

body

claws

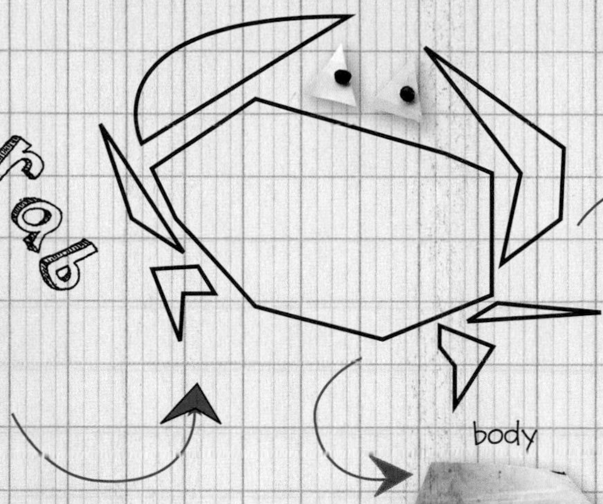

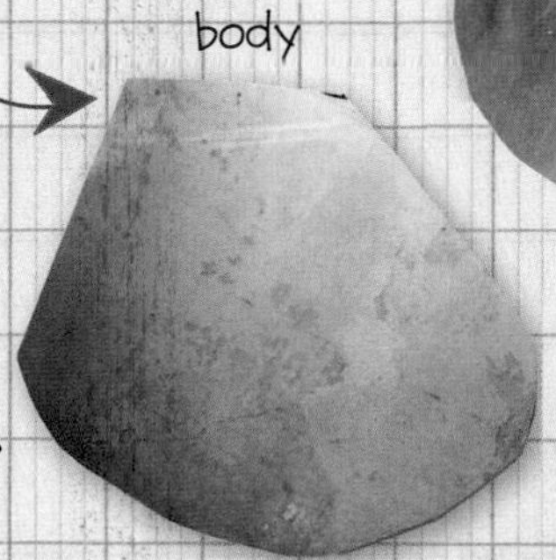

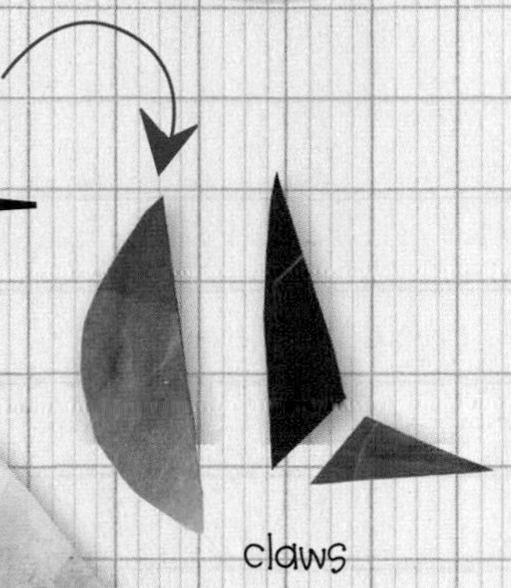

Break down the real shape of a crab into simple shapes. Try to use triangles, half circles, and rectangles. Then cut these out of the magazines.

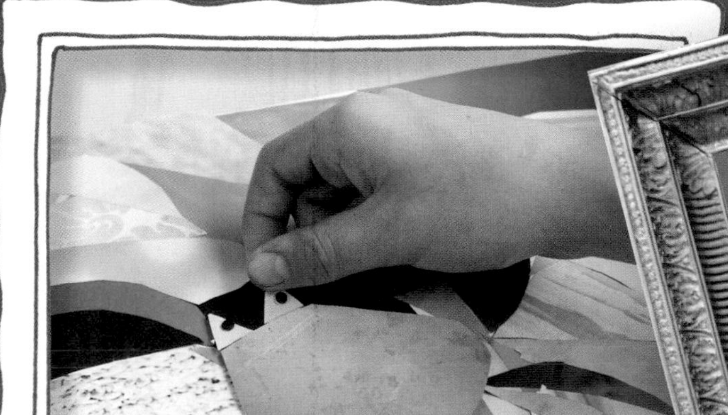

3 Position your crab shape and glue it on the collage. You can also add a few fish. Try matching them to the curves and shapes of the background.

MASTER'S ANIMALS

Here are a few animal-inspired pieces from the legendary artist, Picasso.

The Bull Man Drinking 1958

Picasso used animals and humans as subjects. He also used the half-man, half-bull Minotaur (from Greek mythology) in his paintings.

The Rooster 1943

This painting shows how Picasso would break down an image into simple shapes and colors, without losing the identity of the image—you can still see it's a rooster.

The Bullfight 1934

Bullfights are a traditional pastime in Spain, and Picasso painted dozens of pictures showing the fights' drama and action.

Cat Seizing a Bird
1939

Picasso painted in many different styles during his long career. In the 1930s, he was influenced by the strangeness of surrealism, but he still captured the realities of life, as in _Cat Seizing a Bird_.

Picasso often used scrap materials in his sculptures. The ribs of the goat were made from a wicker basket. It was covered in plaster and then cast in bronze.

She-Goat 1950

From the 1940s, Picasso started to turn his artistic talents to making ceramics. The _Wood-Owl_ is actually a painted ceramic pitcher.

Wood-Owl 1968

Cool cats

BEFORE HE BECAME A FAMOUS pop artist in the 1960s, Andy Warhol (1928-1987) was an illustrator. He loved cats, and in 1954 he published a limited-edition book of drawings called *25 Cats Name Sam and One Blue Pussy*.

25 Cats Name Sam and One Blue Pussy
by Andy Warhol, **1954,**
hand-colored lithograph

Each print is this
big!

Silly numbers

Despite its title, Warhol's book contains only these 16 cats named Sam. (Can you find one with a baby Sam?). There are no words except for labels, done by Warhol's mother. When she was working on the cover, she wrote the title as "25 Cats Name Sam..." instead of "25 Cats Named Sam..." Warhol really liked random mistakes, though—in drawing and in writing—so he left the title that way.

"I never wanted to be a painter. I wanted to be a tap dancer." ANDY WARHOL

Warhol admired the work of American wildlife photographer Walter Chandoha, and owned a book of his cat images. Many of these drawings seem to be inspired by Chandoha's work, as well as by the painter's pets.

Experts think that *One Blue Pussy* is a portrait of one of Warhol's favorite cats, who had recently died. She was named Hester.

INK DOGS

You will need:

Thick paper
Pencil
Pencil eraser
Black felt-tip pen
Watercolor inks
Paint brush

Concentrated inks

Tip:
You only need to add a few drops of ink into a mixing palette, then dilute with water. Remember to test your color on scrap paper before you start painting.

A mixing palette helps to keep your colors separate.

Draw a Dog

Rather than trying to copy Andy Warhol's cats, why not try the same approach with a dog? The outline of a dog is easy to draw if you divide it into simple shapes.

Start with the dog's body. See how it gradually widens from the tail to the rib cage. Now add block shapes for the neck and head.

Finally, add circles for the hips, shoulders, and head. Then straight lines for the legs and feet.

1 Before you start, it's a good idea to practice drawing the shape of your dog on scrap paper.

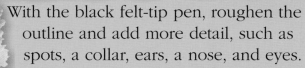

2 When you are ready, draw a pencil outline of your dog on the thick paper. Then go over your outline with a black felt-tip pen and erase the pencil lines.

3 With the black felt-tip pen, roughen the outline and add more detail, such as spots, a collar, ears, a nose, and eyes.

5 Your finished dog should look simple and bold. You can add a little friend for your dog, or try drawing some other animals if you'd like.

4 Choose an ink color and fill inside the outline, or get a friend to help (Warhol held drawing parties and his guests colored each cat).

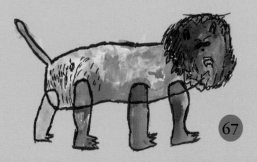

WILD IDEAS

Warhol is famous for movie stars and soup cans, but he also cared about animals.

Grevy's zebra

Danger ahead

It was at the very start of his career, before he became famous, that Andy Warhol drew a collection of charming cats for his friends and family (see pages 64–65). But at the end of his life he turned his attention to different kinds of animal—those that have almost disappeared from the Earth. In 1983, Warhol produced 10 powerful screenprints, each portraying one creature—all the pictures shown here come from this series, which is called *Endangered Species*. In 1986, the year before he died, he published 16 more screenprints of similar subjects in a book called *Vanishing Animals*.

Orangutan

African elephant

To highlight these animals, Warhol used the same kind of harsh, artificial colors that made his pop-art portraits so striking.

Bald eagle

Bighorn ram

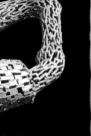

Animals for all

ANDY SCOTT (b. 1964) makes public art. His enormous animals are found all over the world—always in places where lots of people can see them.

This beast, called *Ginger*, was inspired by a dray horse that lived near the artist's home. Dray horses are powerful animals that pull carts.

These sculptures are beautiful, but they still involve the same heavy cutting and welding as industrial metalwork.

Woven steel

All Scott's works are made of steel. First, he builds a sturdy frame, then he welds onto it small sections of steel bar, which look almost like weaving. He then adds small lengths of steel in different shapes and diameters, depending on the size of the sculpture and how delicate each section will be. To make eyelashes, for example, he attaches tiny, narrow pieces.

"So many artists have portrayed animals—I love using hard materials to give them character and movement."

ANDY SCOTT

The real story

Installed outside a veterinary clinic in South Australia, this work—*Loaded Dog*—illustrates a short story by Henry Lawson. In it, a dog named Tommy loves to play fetch, but he gets into trouble when, instead of a piece of wood, he fetches a stick of dynamite.

Heavy Horse
by Andy Scott, **1997,**
galvanized steel

The sculpture is
this **big!**

Artist

This horse, Scott's first
major work, stands 15ft
(4.5m) tall and overlooks a
major highway in Scotland.

MONKEY ON A WIRE

You will need:

Pencil and paper
Cardboard
Pen and sticky tack
Garden wire and pliers
Masking tape
Paints

You can use spray
or acrylic paint.

Be very careful when using the wire.
If you need help always ask an adult.

1 Sketch out the shape of your monkey. Plan the frame of the body. You can copy a monkey from a book and break it down into simple shapes.

2 Use a pen to pierce a hole in the cardboard (position the sticky tack underneath). Feed the end of the wire through the hole and tape it, as shown.

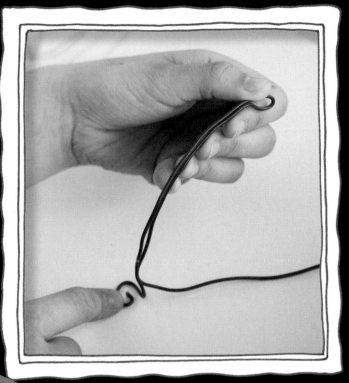

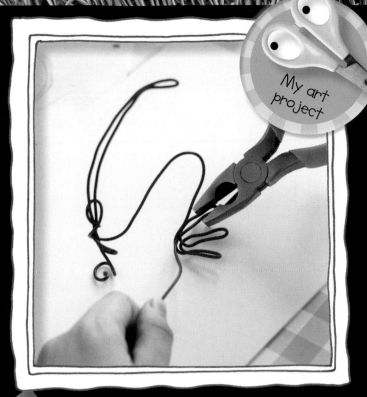

3 Start with the monkey's spine. Create a curved loop in the wire. It's easier to use long pieces of wire—remember to be careful with the sharp ends.

4 From the spine you can form the monkey's legs and feet. If you need to use a new piece of wire, use pliers to hook it around the bottom of the spine.

5 Sculpt the basic shape of your monkey. From the legs you can add the tail. From the spine you can create the monkey's body and arms.

6 Create the head by sculpting several vertical circles and then one horizontal circle around the middle. Use small pieces of wire to add the ear shapes.

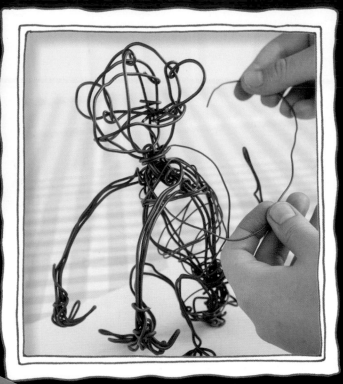

Giraffe

Why not try different animals, such as a tall giraffe or a tiny mouse!

7 Start winding wire around the basic monkey frame. Start with a crisscross pattern around the body and don't pull the wire too tight.

8 Wind the wire around the arms and legs. If you are finding it tricky, you can use the pliers. Finally, finish by twisting the wire around the head.

You can also paint the base.

9 As a finishing touch, you can paint your sculpture silver. If you use spray paints you need to have an adult to do it for you; always use spray paint outside, where it is well ventilated.

Before   After

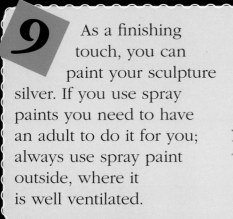

Mouse

Remember to make sure any sharp ends are bent inside the model!

Bend the arms and hook the fingers so your monkey can hold on to things.

Monkey

The tail can be delicate so be careful when you paint and display your model!

ANIMAL SHAPES

Some artists try to portray impressions rather than accurate details.

Pablo Picasso liked to make art out of everyday objects. Here, the crane's head is an old faucet, and the legs are made of forks—the prongs look like toes.

Balloon Dog (yellow) 1994–2000

American artist Jeff Koons made lots of *Balloon Dog* sculptures in different colors, sizes, and materials. This stainless-steel version is about 10ft (3m) high.

Head of a Bull 1943

Picasso needed only two parts of an old bicycle to make this bull's head—the handlebars are the horns, and the seat is the head.

Beast Alerted 1990

Using his skills as a metalworker as well as an artist, Lynn Chadwick tried to show how animals feel. Does this bronze creature look peaceful or panicked to you?

Mammoth 2008

In the California desert, Mexican-American sculptor Ricardo Breceda has created a herd of life-sized prehistoric beasts. Most of his figures, like this mammoth (early elephant), are made in sheet metal with recycled parts added on.

Bird 1959

Henry Moore was inspired to create this bronze figure by watching an injured crow that came to drink at his birdbath.

Glossary

acrylic paint
A type of paint popular since the 1950s. It looks like oil paint, but it's mixed with water and dries more quickly.

canvas
A cloth that artists paint on, usually made of linen or cotton.

collage
A picture made by sticking assorted materials to paper or cardboard.

engraving
A print made from a block that has a design cut or carved on it.

Expressionism
A style of painting where the artist shows emotions and feelings by painting distorted or exaggerated objects rather than realistic ones.

fresco
A painting done in watercolor onto wet plaster. The paint sinks into the plaster as it dries.

gouache
A type of watercolor that is mixed with a special gluelike substance.

hieroglyphs
A small picture of an object that represents a word, sound, o ridea.

lithograph
A print in which the design is drawn with a greasy crayon onto a slab of special stone.

mask
A face covering that hides people's identity, or helps them look like something or someone else.

mosaic
A picture or pattern made up of thousands of tiny pieces, usually of glass or stone.

oil paint
Paint in which the colors are mixed with sticky oils from plants or other sources. It is a favorite with artists, since it can create many different effects.

pastel
A stick of dried paint made from powdered color. It is like a crayon, but not greasy.

pattern
A decorative design.

pigment
Powdered color mixed with liquid to make paint.

Pop art
A type of art that uses bold images like those in comics or advertising.

portrait
A picture or sculpture of a person, especially the face.

screenprint
A print made by wiping ink through a silk mesh onto paper or canvas. Parts of the mesh block the ink to make the design.

sculpture
Art made in three dimensions, usually from materials such as stone, wood, metal, or plastic.

sketch
A rough drawing that acts as a plan for a piece of art.

symbol
A sign or object that stands for something else. For example, lions in paintings may be used to represent royalty.

texture
The look and feel of the surface of a material.

watercolor
A type of paint in which solid colors are mixed with water, then applied with a brush.

woodblock print
A print made from a design that has been carved onto a block of wood. A different wood block is used for each color required.

Index

Acknowledgments

The publisher would like to thank the following for their kind permission to reproduce their photographs:
(Key: a-above; b-below/bottom; c-center; f-far; l-left; r-right; t-top)

2 The Trustees of the British Museum: (t). **Corbis:** The Print Collector (b). **3 The Bridgeman Art Library:** Pushkin Museum, Moscow, Russia/Giraudon (br); Walker Art Gallery, National Museums Liverpool (tl). **V&A Images/Victoria and Albert Museum, London:** (tr). **4 Artothek:** Private Collection. Photo Hans Hinz (cl). **The Bridgeman Art Library:** Scottish National Gallery of Modern Art, Edinburgh, UK/© Succession Picasso/DACS, London 2011. (tl). **Andy Scott:** Hanneke van Wel (br). **Sotheby's, Inc., New York:** © 2011 The Andy Warhol Foundation for the Visual Arts/ARS, NY/DACS, London (tr). **6 The Trustees of the British Museum. 7 Alamy Images:** Ivy Close Images (t). **Corbis:** Bojan Brecelj (c, br). **12-13 Fotolia:** arquiplay77 (background). **12 The Art Archive:** Gianni Dagli Orti (bl). **Getty Images:** DEA/G. Dagli Orti (tr). **Photo Scala, Florence:** Egyptian Museum, Cairo (tr). **13 The Art Archive:** Gianni Dagli Orti (tl). **The Bridgeman Art Library:** Ancient Art and Architecture Collection Ltd. (bl). **Getty Images:** De Agostini (r). **14 Corbis:** The Print Collector. **14-15 Corbis:** The Print Collector (t). **15 Alamy Images:** Interfoto (t, bl). **Corbis:** The Print Collector (crb). **Fotolia:** Carlos Caetano (cr). **18-19 Fotolia:** arquiplay77 (background). **18 akg-images:** Erich Lessing (l). **Getty Images:** (tr); The Bridgeman Art Library (br). **19 akg-images:** Joseph Martin (br). **Alamy Images:** The Art Gallery Collection (tr). **Getty Images:** The Bridgeman Art Library (tl). **21 The Trustees of the British Museum:** (br). **Getty Images:** (bl). **TopFoto.co.uk:** Fine Art Images/Heritage Images (t, tr). **Getty Images:** Erich Lessing (tr). **The Bridgeman Art Library:** By Kind Permission of the Chequers Trust/Mark Fiennes (br, bl). **27 akg-images:** Electa (br). **The Bridgeman Art Library:** Samuel Courtauld Trust, The Courtauld Gallery, London, UK (bl). **Photo Scala, Florence:** © 2011. White Images (t). **28 The Bridgeman Art Library:** The British Sporting Art Trust (bl); Walker Art Gallery, National Museums Liverpool (c, tl). **29 The Bridgeman Art Library:** Walker Art Gallery, National Museums Liverpool. **30 The Bridgeman Art Library:** Walker Art Gallery, National Museums Liverpool (tr). **32-33 Fotolia:** arquiplay77 (background) **32 The Bridgeman**

Art Library: Manchester Art Gallery, UK (l); Private Collection (t); Yale Center for British Art, Gift of Paul Mellon, USA (br). **33 The Bridgeman Art Library:** National Gallery, London, UK. (tl); Yale Center for British Art, Paul Mellon Collection, USA (bl); Private Collection (r). **34-35 V&A Images/Victoria and Albert Museum, London:** (tl, b, tr). **42-43 Fotolia:** arquiplay77 (background). **42 The Bridgeman Art Library:** Frances Broomfield/Portal Gallery, London (br). **Corbis:** Images.com/Ricco/Maresca Gallery, New York (tr). **43 The Bridgeman Art Library:** Private Collection (tl). **Corbis:** The Print Collector (tr). **Gertrud Kanu:** LAVA, Laboratory for Visionary Architecture (br). **LAVA, Laboratory for Visionary Architecture, www.l-a-v-a.net:** Patrick Bingham Hall (cl). **44 The Bridgeman Art Library:** Pushkin Museum, Moscow, Russia/Giraudon. **45 akg-images:** (tl). **The Bridgeman Art Library:** Pushkin Museum, Moscow, Russia/Giraudon (cr). **Corbis:** Alexander Burkatovski (br); Albert Knapp (l). **The Bridgeman Art Library:** Van der Heydt Museum, Wuppertal, Germany (br). **Corbis:** The Gallery Collection (t). **48-49 Fotolia:** arquiplay77 (background). **49 The Bridgeman Art Library:** Kunsthalle, Mannheim, Germany/Interfoto (t); Stadtische Galerie im Lenbachhaus, Munich, Germany/Interfoto (r); Private Collection (bl). **50-51 Artothek:** Private Collection. Photo Hans Hinz. **52 Artothek:** Private Collection. Photo Hans Hinz (br). **56-57 Fotolia:** arquiplay77 (background). **56 The Bridgeman Art Library:** The Israel Museum, Jerusalem, Israel/Gift of the Artist/© Succession Picasso/DACS, London 2011 (cl); Private Collection/Photo © Boltin Picture Library (bl). **Corbis:** © 2011 The Andy Warhol Foundation for the Visual Arts/ARS, NY/DACS, London (br); Alfredo Dagli Orti/The Art Archive (t). **57 The Bridgeman Art Library:** Private Collection/© ADAGP, Paris and DACS, London 2011 (tl); Real Monasterio de El Escorial, El Escorial, Spain (br). **Corbis:** Jacqui Hurst (tr). **Joe Pogan:** Photo Willy Paul (bl). **58 The Bridgeman Art Library:** Scottish National Gallery of Modern Art, Edinburgh, UK/© Succession Picasso/DACS,

London 2011. **59 akg-images:** ullstein bild (tc). **62-63 Fotolia:** arquiplay77 (background). **62 The Bridgeman Art Library:** Private Collection/James Goodman Gallery, New York, USA/© Succession Picasso/DACS, London 2011 (bl). **Getty Images:** Superstock/© Succession Picasso/DACS, London 2011 (br). **Photo Scala, Florence:** Mougins, Picasso Collection/© Succession Picasso/DACS, London 2011 (t). **63 Alamy Images:** Lamb (bl/pedestal). **Christie's:** © Succession Picasso/DACS, London 2011 (bl). **Corbis:** The Gallery Collection/© Succession Picasso/DACS, London 2011 (t). **Photo Scala, Florence:** © 2011 Digital image, The Museum of Modern Art, New York/© Succession Picasso/DACS, London 2011(br). **64-65 Sotheby's, Inc.:** 2011 Tobias Meyer, principal auctioneer, #9588677 © 2011 The Andy Warhol Foundation for the Visual Arts/ARS, NY/DACS, London. **66 S. Moore Photography:** (br). **67 S. Moore Photography:** (tl, tr, bl, cr) **68 Corbis:** © 2011 The Andy Warhol Foundation for the Visual Arts/ARS, NY/DACS, London. Courtesy Ronald Feldman Fine Arts, New York/www.feldmangallery.com (tr, br). **69 Corbis:** © 2011 The Andy Warhol Foundation for the Visual Arts/ARS, NY/DACS, London. Courtesy Ronald Feldman Fine Arts, New York/www.feldmangallery.com/© DACS 2011 (bc, t, bl); **Rex Features:** Nils Jorgensen (br). **70 Andy Scott:** Caroline Scott (tl); Nisbet Wylie Photographs (tc); Hanneke van Wel (bl). **71 Andy Scott:** Hanneke van Wel. **76 Alamy Images:** Sandra Baker/Jeff Koons (l). **Photo Scala, Florence:** BPK, Bildagentur fuer Kunst, Kultur und Geschichte, Berlin/© Succession Picasso/DACS, London 2011 (r). **77 The Bridgeman Art Library:** Private Collection (tr). **Getty Images:** Courtesy Ricardo A Breceda (cr). **Photo Scala, Florence:** Reproduced by permission of The Henry Moore Foundation (br); © 2011. White Images/© Succession Picasso/DACS, London 2011 (tl)

Jacket images: Front: **Alamy Images:** Albert Knapp bl.

All other images © Dorling Kindersley
For further information see: www.dkimages.com